Tough Love / Love

Cynthia Haggans

authorHOUSE®

AuthorHouse™
1663 Liberty Drive
Bloomington, IN 47403
www.authorhouse.com
Phone: 1-800-839-8640

Published by AuthorHouse   03/23/2012

ISBN: 978-1-4567-2303-3 (sc)
ISBN: 978-1-4567-2306-4 (e)

Library of Congress Control Number: 2011900637

This book is printed on acid-free paper.

Acknowledgements

This book is dedicated to all of the wonderful people that God has placed in my life to be an inspiration and assist me along with this project.

I love you dearly; my hubby; Bobby L Haggans, my grand daughter: Chynna and my oldest daughter; Christina.

Last, but not least, my baby girl Chrisiona.

I know that God has nothing but great things for this family.

Your tomorrow is brighter and bigger than your today

Thank you, mom Sandy and J. Cook

I would like to send a shout out to my girl. You have always had an ear for me. I thank you for being my friend, even until this very day.

I love you

G. Cherry

Cynthia Haggans

Contents

Introduction

I must share his goodness in such a time as this.

I know that it look and it sounds like God is
no longer healing, no longer delivering, no
longer opening blind eyes, no longer setting the
whoremonger free, no longer supplying the needs
for his people. As you read this book I hope and
trust in the Lord that you see he is God and he
never changes but we do. He came to set the
captives free.

People such as you and I, the drug dealers
whoremongers, homosexuals blinded eyes, the
lame, etc...

Chapter One

God Knows

I give thanks to the Lord of my life who has inspired me to write this book. I did not quite understand it in the beginning why the Lord would have me to write this book. As the days prolonged, I realized that the very thing God has brought me through, was never really about me. He allowed me to see that it was to benefit someone else.

With all that being said, if you find yourself reading this book then it was you that God had in mind. I went through the storm and the rain, but I trusted In the name of Jesus. This is the reason the name of this book is Tough Love.

Truly, His love kept my mind in perfect peace. His love made me smile when I should have been crying. His love assured me that this too shall pass. God's undeniable love is what saved us. God's love is the reason he sent his son Jesus to the cross who died for us that we might have eternal life.

God says he chastens those whom he loves. When we step out of His will, He chastises us. This is what he will have us to do with our children. Tough love is for that person that you love who does things that may cause you or your family shame, headaches, sleepless night, and stress.

Your marriage may be going south because you are enabling your love one. You may be about to loose what God has blessed you with because of what your love one is going through. Whatever you do, please do not be an enabler.

I want to let you know that an enabler is just what it says it is. When you give money to that love one that has an addiction, you are helping him or her get their next drink or high.

For example, when you have that daughter that does not listen, she goes out and brings a baby home, then you find yourself always taking care of the baby, you are enabling her and she eventually will bring you another one home.

Yes, I had to go there because its time for us to stop enabling our love ones. Tough Love is the best love you can give to the ones we hold dear. Turn them over to Jesus because he has a love that will never fail.

When my son was in high school he was the type that liked to hang out in the streets every day after school not to mention with the wrong crowd. Sometimes he would not come home until two or three o'clock in the morning. When it was time for him to get up for school, it was a struggle for him to get out of bed. I would say, "Son, you cannot hang out all night and expect to be successful in school, it's just not going to work." As time passed, I knew that my son had started smoking but he would never do it in my home. There were times when I would smell alcohol on his breath as well.

I was not just a mother to my son, I was a woman who loved the Lord, and He was first in my life. I was a praying mother, one who labored in prayer on behalf of my children and others. I lived a God fearing life before my children.

Not to mention I had gone through an abusive marriage for ten plus years. For ten plus years I was beaten. When I say beaten, I was thrown around the house as if I was another male. There were times when I was kicked and spat upon. I was often told that I would never amount to nothing and would never be anybody. I was constantly told that I was stupid most of the time and called a whore everyday.

One day I removed my child and myself away from all of the madness. How many of you know that does not always help? I was in my new place of residence one day and he, my ex-husband, was at the door. He spoke with a very kind voice, he said he needed to ask me a question, and so I opened the door. I allowed him in and my phone rang. He asked who was calling. I realized at this point in my life that I would not allow this monster to control me any longer.

I asked him to leave my apartment and of course that did not go over too well with that ***MONSTER!***

He jumped up and grabbed me. I fought this brother back. He was angry. We ended up in the hallway of my apartment. on the floor, he held my neck with a firm grip and shoved my head into the wall. I am sharing this with you because as a women we sometimes will accept anything and call it love. This is not LOVE!

This is not what God intended for you as a woman.

It is not God's will for your children to have to live in such nightmare.

Often times, women do not tell when they are in an abusive relationship. Why? I do not know. Maybe you are a shamed. This would be the perfect reason to remove yourself and let someone know that you are being abused.

I was not willing to keep it a secret. First of all this is something that will make the news quickly with me being the victim. This is why I exposed this monster. Everybody needs to know for safety reasons.

I would call the cops. I told my pastor. I felt as though he needed to know what kind of demon he had as president of his Usher board.

During this ten-year span, not only did I experience abuse, but also I lost my mother. As I said early on, God's love kept me through the mist of my storms.

Do not forget God had you in mind. While having issues with a delinquent son, an abusive husband, the death of my mother, a separation, and a year later a divorce! I must say that I now am very grateful that he chose me to endure this.

One Thursday night during the fall, I showered
and got dressed for church and during the fall,
it is nice during the day but at night, it is cool. I
looked in my closet for a jacket to wear I had all
kind of coats from maxi leather, cashmere, short
leather, etc... to my surprise I could not find one,
not a one. My heart was so heavy I could not cry.
I pulled myself together got dressed and went out
to church. This monster had stole every coat that
I had.

God loves us so much that he always prepares
a vessel for the storms. God wants you to know
that what he has done for me he will do for you
also. As I write this book, the Holy Spirit bring
all things back to my memory. I recall having a
conversation with the Lord one night after bible
class about Judas, the one that betrayed Jesus
and the Lord said to me I had to prepare a body
for this very thing so that I could go to the cross
for my people.

If Judas had not betrayed him, there would not
have been a crucifixion. Wow, what I am saying
is he had to use a body for this very storm and it

was me. I pray that as you read this book it will increase your faith, and strengthen your walk with the Lord.

If you do not know him as your personal savior, I trust that you will invite him into your heart, mind, and soul. Parents this one is for you! We as parents really need to converse with our children frequently to find out what is on your children's mind. I believe that kids act out when something is lacking in the home. If you are a single parent, it could be that your child wants to be with the absent parent. If you work all the time, it could be that they just want you to come home, fix dinner and take them out to do something fun.

I came out of a home with a single parent. My father walked out and abandoned us. Leaving my mother with four boys and three girls to raise alone. I was the fourth eldest and the only girl for a long time. I felt alone as I got older because I needed someone to talk to. I did not have that person in my life to communicate with, as I became a teenager. I always wondered about life in general. I had questions like, why did my father abandon us or why did I feel so unloved?

My mother was always there for us. She had so many kids to take care of that she felt that the younger ones needed her the most. I can truly say that I suffered from a lack of attention.

I lost out in the area of teen talk. I went to people who were much older than I and were not believers in the Lord. All they did was drink Mr. Richards, Mr. Boone's Farm. I must say I thank God for deliverance because the whole drinking thing was not for me. As a reminder, this is what happens when you do not have quality time for your little ones. They will go to someone or something.

Chapter Two

Through The Storm

One Saturday night around 12:00am in the early 90's, a terrible thunderstorm came. I was about to say my prayers before getting in bed. I tucked my 6-year-old daughter in bed and prayed "Lord you said in your word that a child that does not obey his father or mother will shorten his days here on earth. I said you have no respect of persons, I give my son to you on this night, what ever you see fit to happen in his life just give me the strength to say Amen to your will God."

I cried for about an hour that night. It seemed like the thunder got louder and louder, and then lightening came. I had no idea where my child was in the mist of this terrible storm. All I knew is that I wanted him home after all; he was only 18 years old at this time.

As a mother and a single mother at that, I had nothing but love in my heart for my child. When he did finally come home, from being out all night, he would sleep all day. During this time, I was trying to figure out "What could a person be involved in that it would take all night long to do?" I never did come up with the answer. I told him that he could not hang out all night, come into my house, and sleep all day. It hurt me inside to know that his 6-year-old sister did not have the big brother that she should have. She needed a big brother to teach her to ride a bike, play kick ball, learn how to roller skate; walk her to the pool and teach her to swim. At this time I was divorced, had gone back to school and had a new job at the hospital working second shift.

With the Lord's help of course, I was ready to take care of my two kids in our new apartment.

My daughter was seven or eight years old at that time. I talked to my son about taking care of his little sister until I returned home from work. I did not know that his addiction was so severe that he could not stay off the block long enough to make sure that his sister was cared for. He would leave her unattended and she would call my job crying because she was alone. This would just break my heart. The very last time it happened, I walked away from my job that I loved so much. As a mother, I could not stand the thought of her being alone. My Lord blessed me again with a job during the hours she was in school. Red was not willing to help with his little sister while I worked to take care of them.

As his mother, one day I had to except that he was an addict this is what they do.

Since I did not know how serious his addiction was, I tried another plan with him.

I gave him two options he had to either to get a job or go back to school because it was time that he did something to improve himself.

During this time, he also had a child that he needed to support. A year later on top of all I was going through with him, he had another baby. For two years, I was angry inside wondering why all of this happened to me. Why was I being hit with one storm after the next?

There was a young woman that my son was overtaken by; I think he would have jumped out of a window for her. You all know how that is, right? She was the one who gave me the inside scoop on crack cocaine and how it affected you. I was devastated by the information that I had to take a leave of absence from work.

In dealing with all of this, I still had my daughter to take care of. I did all I could do to get my daughter ready and out the door for school. I lay in my apartment and cried for weeks. Once getting my daughter off to school, I would return to my apartment, fall on my knees, and cry out to the Lord for help. I reminded myself of the poor man in the book of Psalms, that cried out and how God delivered him out of all of his troubles.

At this time in my life, all I wanted is for this storm to be over. Once while my son was home, I asked him to please go out and find a job, and his response to me was "I'm not doing nothing!" I became furious and fed up at this point. I went in his bedroom and piece by piece, I took his bedroom suite down. I took it outside and placed it against my apartment. Within weeks some young lady with a child stopped by and asked how much I was selling the bedroom furniture for. I sold it to her for $75.00 dollars. God had given me strength I needed in order to give him tough love. I did not have this strength at first but I looked him in his eyes and said, "Son I don't know what's going on but I did not raise you like this and I refuse to raise your sister in this type of environment!" The smell of drugs, cigarette smoke, and alcohol had to go.

I was not going to allow him to bring that in my home any longer since he was not willing to make any changes to better himself. I meant that. Wherever he was getting the drugs from he had to live there. It hurt beyond measure to have to put my son out of my house, but I stood my ground. I realized at this time that you could not play with the devil.

Through all of this, it drew me closer to God in prayer and fasting. I had one girlfriend that I would talk to about what I was up against. I use to get so tired of not having anything different to tell. I would go days without talking to her. I realized without her,

all I had was the Lord and my children whom I love.

By 1993 things got somewhat better for me. My son was about 22 years old and would stay away from home for days. I was no longer staying in bed crying. God had given me a spirit of peace at this time. The peace that He said would pass all understanding.

He then started going to jail. I would get up early Saturday mornings to get downtown to make the visitation hours, and leave or send checks for commissary while he was in jail, and excepted those expensive collect calls. This went on for two years. Of course, this meant that he was only getting older and so was I.

So once again, I told him, if this is what he wanted for his life I could not support him any longer. So of course, he had not gotten tired of this cycle. He continued to do drugs and go to jail. It got to the point when he went to jail he would call his friend collect and she would perform three-way on her line to call to me.

This way there were not charges for collect calls on my bill. He would let me know his court date and the public defender that was appointed to him.

I felt in my heart that jail was the best place for my son. I knew exactly where he was. He was safe and not getting high. He ate three times a day. I also knew that he was not sleeping in the streets. I always hoped that once released he would not go back to doing drugs, but that never happened. I always made his court dates awaiting his appearance in the courtroom. I never wanted the judge to think that he was just another black male in the system that did not have anyone who loved him.

It seem like every time he would go before the judge he would have a bible from the jail in his hand holding it like he just believed God was going to get him out of his mess. Lo and behold, he would get "time served" and he would get released from jail. I would leave the courthouse thinking he will be home soon. Oh, but I would be so wrong. He always made his way from the jail to the block. I remember telling him once that someone could drive by the block and shoot everyone standing there and no one would never know who did it and why?

You know that went over his head because he never stopped hanging out.

Chapter Three

No Man Can Pluck You Out

One day shortly after I buried my mother, I
was at work and I received a phone call from a
police officer. He said "Ms. Barnes this is Officer
Jones from the county police department". My
heart immediately dropped, he said, "I'm calling
because your son has been shot". I asked, "Where
is he?" and he told me that my son was in the
hospital. I pulled myself together. When I got
there the Lord spared his life!. He could have
easily been killed due to the lifestyle he chose

to live. I must say the very block that I spoke
to him about, the very wisdom I had spoken to
him, he allowed to go over his head. Yes, it really
happened just the way I said it would happen.
Once arriving to the hospital my son was awake
and conscience. I had a million questions to ask
him all in one breathe. What happened? I asked,
"Who did this to you?"

Why? I had so many questions that needed
answers. He had been shot twice, once in the
leg and once in the upper back, while he was
running from the gunman. I began to tell him
that it was God that kept him alive. The bullet
that went through the back of his shoulder
could have easily been the back of his head. It
could have easily been his spine, but the hand
of God was there even through it all. He had
been assaulted more than six times. Once he
had been beaten so bad that he could not tell the
young women that stopped to help him his name,
someone else who saw the assault told the young
women where he lived.

My daughter and I were at home in the bed
on this particular Friday night. It was around
12:00am that I heard a knock at the door, and
when I opened the door, there were two young
women on each side of my son.

He could not even walk, they had to act as
crutches for him to get him up stairs in my
apartment he was beaten just that bad.

The night before I had gone to get his tuxedo,
he had been asked to go to the senior prom with
a nice young lady from the High school where
he attended. It saddened my heart to know that
because of the life he had chosen, he missed a
memorable event at his high school prom. Not
only that but at the last minute this young lady
wouldn't have a date.

Once I got him in the house, I had to get my
daughter out of bed, dress her, and get my son
to the emergency room to be treated. I had to
go through all of this for him to rest for the
remainder of the day and find himself back out on

the block the following day using crack cocaine and drinking alcohol. I kept him soaked in prayer and never gave up. I WAS CRAZY ENOUGH TO BELIEVE GOD'S WORD, for my son to be free from that witchcraft spirit. I know longer wanted to enable him. I wanted him to know that God had something greater for his life and the devil came to kill, to steal, and to destroy his life.

I told my family, a long time ago, "As for me and my house, we will serve the Lord."

Chapter Four

Gotta' Move On

Between the years of 1994-95, I had turned over a new page in my life and concerning my son. I packed our things and moved from my apartment. I did not try to find my son to let him know that I had moved and did not want him to have my new address. I was done. I did not want to have anything to do with him. It was not him that I did not want to deal with per say, but it was that witchcraft spirit of drugs that I did not want to deal with.

I was tired of the life style he had chosen. It had gotten so bad that every time he came around something would leave with him. He would steal my money that I had for the week or my daughter's bike. He would ask her if he could borrow it to ride to the store and she would say "yes". I mean, what more can you expect from a young child that loves her big brother. He would never return with it.

This happened twice. I bought her a Nintendo for Christmas one year only to come home to find it missing. I never saw it again. He stole my car. I could not endure that pain any longer. The pain of knowing that my son whom I took care of and raised to the best of my ability and with the help of God, turned out to be this person that I didn't know.

He was a person that would take from me, his own mother, my daughter, his only sister in order to feed this monster of crack, this was my son, and that reality hurt me so bad.

The reality of knowing that as a parent, at this time, he had three of his own and did not try to take care of them, hurts beyond words.

Someone I knew had given him the address of where I moved, and not long after finding out where I was, he broke into my house through a window when I was not home. I pressed charges against him and he spent six months in prison.

That was **tough love**. It killed me inside to press charges against him, but it was necessary. I loved my son and I wanted him sober and not controlled by substances. Upon his release, not surprisingly, he got out and did the same thing all over again.

Back to the streets he had gone. I had to ban him from my house, and he was shot again and through prayer he over came that. After that wind blew over, in came baby number five. They were twins, so now he had five children and was not taking care of any of them.

He met a young lady and did well for a few weeks, then he would come up missing. This meant that he had relapsed and went back to using crack. This time when he went back out there, I received notification that he'd been hit in the back, right over the kidney with a two by four slab.

The doctors say that if he were hit any lower it would have damaged his kidney. Again, another escape from the death angel, another time God showed his grace and mercy and intervened. He was in the hospital for two weeks from this injury.

Chapter Five

Dirty Laundry

The Sunday morning of July 2002, my daughters
and I were up about to get ready for church, but
before we went to church I needed to run to the
grocery store to pick something up for dinner
after church.

My daughter Cole, at this time had grown into
a beautiful teenager. I had another experience
another blow in life and had another wonderful
daughter. I opened the garage door to put some

laundry in before leaving the house, only to find the body of a man lying out there beside the washer and dryer.

Lying there still, was my son "Red" and there was blood all over the clothes that had been placed out there to be washed. He finally moved; praise the name of the Lord. I said "Get up now!" and as he struggled to get up I saw a deep womb to his head.

He said in a weak feeble voice "Ma a guy got mad while I was out there and we fought. I was beating him up so he picked up a metal rod and hit me in the head with it". I had to rush to put clothes on and get him to the hospital.

Thank God, it was not too far from our home. I dropped him off at the hospital and I went home and went to church. I knew that only God could fix him. I had done all I could do and all that I knew to do, for him.

After this incident, I tried talking to him once again. I said, "Son you have got to get into a recovery or half way house. He called a few places and finally got into a drug rehabilitation center. He stayed there for two weeks and while there, he obtained a lot of needed information. While there he received information about a half way house that he was interested in going to.

He called them and set up an interview. I took him to his interview. The men there voted him in. I had to pay for him to get started in this facility. This time I did not mind paying, because I knew that it was something to help better the life of my son.

While in this house the men had to work, pay weekly rent, buy their own food, and do daily chores. He had to go to an NA meeting every week. Most importantly, they had to stay clean from alcohol and any illegal drugs.

To God be all the glory! This was the first time in ten years that my son honestly showed any effort of wanting to be clean, and lives a normal life. He stayed in that facility for about four years. He eventually moved up and became president of the house. For the first time in his life, he was dedicated to his job.

He learned the importance of working. He learned how to be independent, and responsible. Between the years of 2005 and 2006, I can truly say that Jesus renewed the mind of my son! For once in his adult life he had positive plans for his himself. He became more active in the lives of his children.

It really shocked me when he took the initiative and went to the State Child Support office and had a certain amount deducted out of his pay check for his children. I knew this time that it was not anything but prayer, **tough love, and love** that got my son to this place in his life.

Chapter Six

Proud Family

He did decide to move out of the half way house. I gave him another chance to move back home with me, and I gave him one month to save for his own apartment. I was so proud of him and his sister was too.

He found him a two-bedroom apartment not too far from my house. He did this in hopes of obtaining full custody of his third child that was taken from her mother and my son due to drugs.

When they initially took her she was given to me as the next of kin, but I was given only temporary custody.

At this time, I was going through another storm in my life and knew that it was not a good idea for me to raise another child at this time. Therefore, I talked to my brother and my sister in law about raising my granddaughter, their great-niece and they agreed because we did not want her in foster care with strangers and she had living and well off family members. We went to court and the judge awarded my brother and his wife full custody of my granddaughter.

However, once the courts saw that my son had cleaned himself up, was living a stable life and had a stable home for his child things really started to look up for him.

In 2007, the state awarded him his daughter. God was good to him even in the mist of his daughter being taken and put in foster care. In most cases, the child is taken and the family looses all rights to these kids, never to be given back to their parents.

Jesus showed Himself again even in this situation
and all I could say is "Thank you Lord for all
you have done, thank you for your love and the
strength you've given me to give my son tough
love!" I know that
"Tough Love" is the reason that he's the man he is
today.

He got his driver's license and a car of his own.
He also owned two cars but sold one. God did it.
He went from stealing my car with no license to
having his own car and driving legal.

Chapter Seven

Just You Believe

The Lord just brought another situation to mind to share with you. I don't share this one too often but I believe it's going to set you free from unbelief.

One summer I was home on break from school, I worked with special needs high school students. I wanted to do something with my time. I decided to sell fish dinners on a Friday because I just love to cook.

My friend and my sister in the Lord came over to buy four dinners from me but she did not come alone. A young lady that I knew because I dated her brother for five years. I had given her and her child a place to stay when her brother put them out of his house in the middle of the night.

I left work one day to look for an apartment for her. The manager agreed to lease her the apartment without her having a job.

All I wanted was for her and her child to have a stable home. At sometime or another she started to smoke crack. Not to mention, you hardly ever saw her without a beer in her hand. That Friday my friend and this young woman left my house. Unfortunately, my pocketbook left too. I realized this, as I was going out the door. My purse was no where to be found.

All the money I had at the time was in my purse. I worked for the state and was paid once a month.

My tithes and offering was in my purse. All I could think about was God's money going up in smoke.

The next morning my cousin Judy and I had a yard sale. My phone rang and it was my friend that purchased the four plates along with the young lady. She said, "I am so sorry that I brought her to your house she stole your purse Cynthia.

This morning I drove to the pharmacy to get my meds and your purse was in my car. I looked in it first to see what was in it. I saw your money and everything looked like it's still in there".

This was the power of God causing a crack head who had access to hundred of dollars to not buy crack.

I really hope my testimony will increase your faith and you will just trust God.

Parents I beg you if you have a child or know of
someone with kids / grandkids encourage that
person to stay on top of the kids. Know who their
teachers are and make sure they know who you
are. Attend meetings at their school. Volunteer
your time at the school, so you can really have a
feel of what is going on in that school.

I worked in the public school system for years
and I have seen some unbelievable things. For
example: a young man use to leave home looking
like a young man, but before first period is over
he was wearing daisy duke shorts and wearing
stilettos. I am talking about age fourteen or
fifteen years of age.

One day it was so bad he was distracting the
class with his wig and attire, they called his
father to come and pick him up. I really felt bad
for this father because your child left home one
way and you find out later that something else is
going on.

Once he got to school he became something he was not. A man will never be a woman but you know that is a another topic. We just have to do as the bible says and that is pray for one another.

It could be the other way. You could be getting a phone call about your child transforming into another creature. Pray always for one another. It is tight but it is right!.

All I can say is Thank you Lord for what you have done for me. My sister or brother do not close your eyes to your surroundings. The bible says to watch as well as to pray. God will show you things while in prayer, in your sleep, or he may have a woman or man of God to tell you the spiritual instructions needed for your life. When that happens just receive it and fix it for your child's sake. Everybody wants his or her children to be successful in life. It starts at home not in the school. It starts at home.

We talk about people not knowing how to love anymore.

Guess what it starts at home than it spreads
aboard.
It is what it is.

A certain song states that we have to clean up
what we've messed up. When I was a kid, we ate
together as a family. My mother would bless the
food and you would speak a bible verse. Whatever
you wanted on the table you would ask may I
have or could you pass me the salt or the pepper.
You would always say thank you.

Before you walked across someone, you had to
say excuse me. If you bumped into someone you
said, excuse me. We really need to get back to the
basics with our children. It is called respect. We
must teach them respect in the home.

Again, it starts in the home.

We must do a better job with them. We are a
strong and intelligent people. Let us get it right
and walk in the blessings God has prepared for
our households.

Pray with your children, pray for them and do not ever give up on them. God can and he will answer your prayers. Just when you think it is not going to happen, it will happen. Our time is not his time and his time is not our time. He is a just and on time God. This thing really works. O' taste and see that the Lord is good.

Because can't nobody do you like Jesus. You can search the world all over and you will not find anyone like him.

If I have never done anything to help my fellowman along the way I trust that something in this book will encourage you, you, and you. I thank you for supporting me. Keep your head up and know that you are somebody in Christ Jesus, I want to encourage that parent that's going through with that child. Hang in there!

Weeping may endure for a night but joy comes in the morning. Just trust God and not man for your morning, it will come. Thank him in advance for it.

Do not wait until the battle is over praise him for it now.

God sees and he knows the pain, the sorrow, and the disappointment, the lies that have been spoken in your ears, all of this is hard and too heavy for you but just right for him. I say to you release it unto the Lord. He will fight your battle every one of them. Jesus loves you just that much.

I love you with the love of the Lord. Without love, we profit nothing.

So to you, I say if you want to help your loved one, prayer and tough love are the answers to get them back to the responsible person they should be. Thank you for your support and reading my book during this special time in my life. Always keep in mind that God have no respectful person. He did it for me he will do it for you.

Whatever you do, do not doubt God he can and he will fix your situation or your tomorrow.

Lean not to your own understanding but I will say acknowledge him in your situation or your tomorrow

Make your request known unto him. When you do, believe that he will answer your cry. Just as he did for me. I want you to know that nothing, nothing, I cannot stress that enough nothing, is too hard for God.

God bless you and your family!

Cynthia Haggans

After this wonderful journey I embarked upon another hidden gift....Poetry. God revealed this unto me in the wee hours in the morning. What a wonderful God we serve!

I really hope you enjoy them!

I WONDER WHY

I WONDER WHY

I WONDER WHY

YOU LOVE ME SO

WHEN I DID NOT KNOW

I WONDER WHY

I WONDER WHY

YOU DIED SO THAT I

CAN BE A LIVE

I WONDER WHY

I WONDER WHY

YOU FORGIVE

WHEN I DID NOT YIELD

I WONDER WHY

I WONDER WHY

YOU SHED YOUR BLOOD

WHEN I was

IN THE MUD

I WONDER WHY

I WONDER WHY

YOU PREPARE A TABLE

WHEN I DIDN'T LABOR

I WONDER WHY

I WONDER WHY

I GUESS I WILL GO ON

WONDERING WHY

UNTIL I DIE

BY CYNTHIA DENISE HAGGANS

Now is the Time

You know yesterday is gone

And the leaves are blown

Our people act like there mind is gone

It's really not your mind

But it is your time

You will be left behind

Being behind is not a good sign

God will deal with your behind

In his own time

Cynthia Denise Haggans